HANDS-ON GEOLOGY

Get Hands-On with Types of Soil!

Alix Wood

Full of real geology experiments that help you learn all about types of soil.

PowerKiDS press.

New York

Published in 2022 by Rosen Publishing
29 East 21st Street, New York, NY 10010

Produced for Rosen Publishing by Alix Wood Books
Designed and illustrated by Alix Wood
Editor: Eloise Macgregor
Consultant: Kate Spencer, Professor of Environmental Geochemistry

Cataloging-in-Publication Data
Names: Wood, Alix.
Title: Get hands-on with types of soil! / Alix Wood.
Description: New York : PowerKids Press, 2022. | Series: Hands-on geology |
Includes glossary and index.
Identifiers: ISBN 9781725331358 (pbk.) | ISBN 9781725331372 (library bound) |
ISBN 9781725331365 (6 pack) | ISBN 9781725331389 (ebook)
Subjects: LCSH: Soils--Juvenile literature. | Soil formation--Juvenile literature.
Classification: LCC S591.3 W66 2022 | DDC 551.3'05--dc23

Photo credits:
Cover, 1, 4 middle, 8 top, 10 top right, 12, 13, 14, 16, 18, 20, 24, 25 top, 26 top, 27 top, 28
top and middle © AdobeStock Images; 11 top © Antonio Jordán; 28 bottom © creative
commons/bobistraveling; all other illustrations @ Alix Wood

Printed in the United States of America

CPSIA Compliance Information: Batch #CSPK22. For Further Information contact Rosen Publishing, New York, New York at 1-800-237-9932.

Contents

What Exactly Is Soil?

Earth is covered by a thin layer known as the **crust**. On the surface of the crust is loose material geologists call soil. Soil forms where the rock mixes with water and air. It contains **organic matter** and helps plants to grow. The inner layers of the Earth do not contain soil. They are made from rock, metals, and gases.

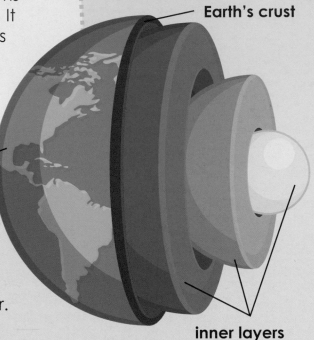

Earth's crust

Soil occurs on the surface of the land on Earth's crust.

inner layers

Soil layers

Soil is a mixture of tiny pieces of rock, dead plants and animals, air, and water. It has many small spaces in it that hold water and air. Soil forms different layers.

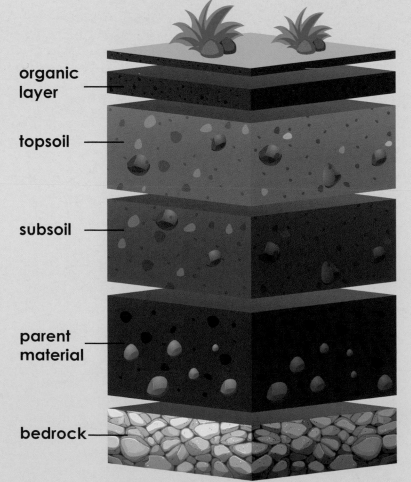

organic layer

topsoil

subsoil

parent material

bedrock

The top layer of soil is made up of organic matter such as rotting leaves and twigs.

Topsoil is made up of organic matter and **minerals**. Plants and **organisms** live in this layer.

Subsoil is made mainly of clay, with very small amounts of organic matter.

This rocky layer is called the parent material layer because the material in this layer creates the layers above.

The layer just beneath soil is known as bedrock. It is several feet below the surface, and is a solid mass of rock.

Why Should We Study Soil?

Soil is more than just dirt. Geologists study soil because it is so important to our planet. It supports life on Earth in many ways!

 Most plants need soil to grow. Soil gives them **nutrients** and helps anchor them into the ground by their roots. Soil also takes **nitrogen** out of the **atmosphere** and converts it into food for plants.

 Soil helps our atmosphere by storing **carbon**. This helps reduce the amount of harmful **carbon dioxide** gas in the air.

 Many living things make their homes in soil.

 The soil helps to filter and clean our water. It also soaks up rain, which protects areas from flooding.

HANDS-ON Examine Your Local Soil

You will need:
- an outside area
- permission to dig there
- a spade or trowel
- a bucket
- a magnifying glass
- tweezers
- black and white paper
- a pen or pencil

Ask an adult if you can dig up a cup of soil from your neighborhood. Dig away from new plants, so you don't just get store-bought soil.

Get a sheet of white and a sheet of black paper. Place some soil on each sheet. The different colors help show up different parts of the soil. Using a magnifying glass, have a close look at the samples. Can you see tiny rocks and sand? Or leaves? Or bits of wood? Is the soil crumbly or clumpy? What does it smell like? Did you find any bugs or worms?

Write down your findings. Keep all your science notes. They will help you identify what type of soil you have later in the book.

Always wash your hands well after handling soil. Bacteria living in soil might make you sick.

How Is Soil Formed?

Soil is a little like a cookie mix, made up of different ingredients. Soil is around 5 percent organic matter, 45 percent minerals, and around 50 percent empty space! The empty space gets filled with air and water. All the parts of the mix arrive in the soil in different ways.

organic matter

minerals and rock

space between the matter fills with air or water

Decaying Organic Matter

In the fall, falling leaves create a carpet of rotting matter. Bugs, such as millipedes, shred the leaves into pieces. Earthworms gather the pieces and pull them under the soil to their burrows. Tiny **microbes** in the soil release **chemicals** that help crumble the organic matter into even smaller pieces. After worms eat the leaves, their poop, known as worm casts, adds more goodness to the soil mix.

What Is in Organic Matter?

- **decomposing** parts of plants such as leaves, twigs, bark, roots, and grass cuttings.
- decomposing dead animals and insects
- tiny, living microbes that help decompose plants and animals
- animal manure

A Dash of Rock and Minerals

Soils are formed by **weathering**. Weathering is the breaking down of rock on the surface of Earth's crust. The solid rock is broken down into tiny pieces by water and ice. How can ice break rock? Water in cracks in the rock freeze and expand, which causes the rock to break. Rainwater can even dissolve solid limestone rock, although the process may take hundreds of years.

Then Add Time!

The final part of your soil recipe is time, and plenty of it. It takes around 500 years for just one inch (2.5 cm) of soil to form! Soil takes longer to form in cold and dry places than in warm and wet regions. Why? Processes such as weathering and rotting happen slower in cold and dry areas. Warmth and water speed up rotting and weathering. Organic matter and microbes need water and warmth to grow, so soil production is much faster if the **climate** is warm and wet.

Think About This...

Rocks and minerals are added to the surface of soil by weathering. How do you think rock from the lower parent rock layer gets added to the topsoil?

BE A SOIL GEOLOGIST
Make Your Own Compost

You Will Need:

adult help needed

- a plastic bottle
- scissors
- some tape
- some moist soil
- a mix of eggshells, kitchen vegetable waste, tea and coffee grounds, grass clippings, and leaves

The Geology:

You can make compost in around three months – a lot quicker than it takes to make soil. The best compost has a mix of brown material, such as old leaves, and green plant material. Soil adds the microbes that help break the mixture down.

How to Make It:

Rinse out the bottle and remove the label. Ask an adult to help cut around the bottle, a third of the way down. Put the top to one side.

Place some moist soil at the base of the bottle. Add a layer of kitchen waste. Then add layers of leaves, grass, eggshells, tea grounds, and coffee grounds. Between each layer add a thin layer of soil.

Tape the top back on to the base. Put the bottle in a sunny place. If it steams up, open the lid to let the compost dry a little. If it looks too dry, add some water. Roll the bottle every day to mix the compost. It is ready when the mixture turns brown and crumbly.

Is All Soil the Same?

Differences in the local rock and the local weather mean that soil can be very different from region to region. There are three basic types of soil particles: sand, **silt**, and clay. Soils are rarely pure sand, silt, or clay but are usually a mixture of all three.

Clay soil is usually sticky with very small, fine **particles**. It contains few air gaps so water does not drain through it easily.

Think About This... ?

This diagram shows the different types of soil that can come from different mixtures of sand, silt, and clay. Loam is a mixture of the three. What do you think loam might feel like?

percent clay

clay

clay

silty clay

sandy clay

clay loam

silty clay loam

sandy clay loam

loamy sand

sandy loam

silt loam

loamy sand

sand

percent silt

sand

percent sand

silt

Sandy soil is pale in color and has large particles. These visible grains create lots of small air gaps between them. Water drains through the gaps easily, so sand usually feels dry.

Silt is made up of fine rock and mineral particles that are slightly larger than clay particles. Silt soil both drains well and holds moisture well.

BE A SOIL GEOLOGIST
How Much Sand? Silt? Clay?

You Will Need:

- three large jars with lids
- soil from three different places
- a marker
- some water softener if you have some

The Geology:

Sand, silt, clay, and organic matter form different layers at different speeds. The biggest particles settle first, therefore they settle in this order: gravel, sand, silt, clay, organic material (which may float on the water!). Not all material may be present in each sample.

How to Do the Experiment:

Fill a jar half full of soil from three different places. Write on the lid where each sample came from using a marker. You should now have three jars all with different soil in them. Wet the soil a little until it looks like mud.

Tap the jars to settle the soil. Mark the level of soil on each jar using a marker. Write "soil" next to each mark.

Put a teaspoon of water softener, if you have some, in each jar. Now fill the jars to the top with water. Put on the lids and shake the jars so the soil and water mix.

Let the soil in the jars settle for one minute. Then mark the level of the layer of settled soil on each jar. This is the sand in your soil samples. Write "sand" next to your marks.

After around an hour, mark the level of the soil again. The difference between the bottom mark and the second mark is the silt in your soil. Label these marks "silt."

After a day, the top clay layer should have settled. Mark this level with a line marked "clay."

Which layers were thickest? Which were thinnest? Was it the same in all your jars? Which kinds of soil do you think you have?

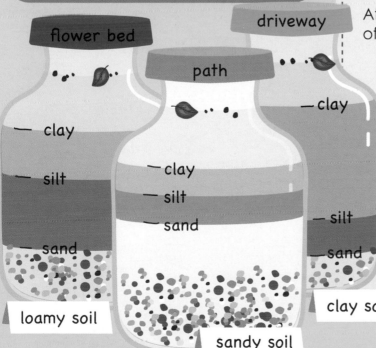

flower bed
driveway
path
— clay
— clay
— clay
— silt
— silt
— silt
— sand
— sand
— sand

loamy soil
sandy soil
clay soil

Making Soil Profiles

Geologists sometimes need to create a soil profile for an area. They might drill with an **auger** into the soil and bring up core samples. These long, tube-shaped samples show what the soil is like at different depths. Each layer of soil is called a horizon. The simplest soils have three horizons.

A horizon

B horizon

C horizon

Topsoil, known as the A horizon, is usually the darkest layer of the soil because it has so much organic material.

Subsoil, known as the B horizon, is where minerals and clays are found. Subsoil is lighter brown and holds more water than the topsoil.

The C horizon contains large pieces of bedrock.

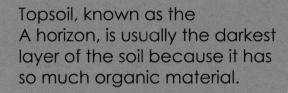

an auger

HANDS-ON Make a Soil Profile Card

You will need:
- a shovel
- card stock
- a pencil
- double-sided tape
- a tape measure
- some paper

Ask permission to dig a very deep hole in some soil. Look for changes in color as you dig. Take samples from different depths and wrap each sample in paper. Write the depth on each sample.

On a piece of card stock, lay a strip of double-sided tape along one edge. Carefully sprinkle each sample, in order, down the strip. Label the depth you found them next to each sample.

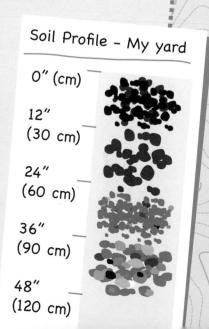

Soil Profile – My yard

0" (cm)

12" (30 cm)

24" (60 cm)

36" (90 cm)

48" (120 cm)

Building on Soil

Geologists are often asked to check soil at construction sites. The construction team needs to be sure the soil will be stable enough to support the weight of any buildings.

Think About This... ?

Why do you think this famous tower in Pisa, Italy, leans over?

BE A SOIL GEOLOGIST
Testing Soil Foundations

You Will Need:

- a tall, unbreakable container
- some rocks, gravel, soil, and sand
- a potato masher
- some books
- masking tape
- a marker
- notebook and pencil

The Geology:

Buildings are built on foundations. How deep those foundations go depends on the size and weight of the building and the type of soil underneath it. Before building on a piece of land, it is important for geologists to draw up a soil profile.

How to Make It:

Put a strip of masking tape up the side of the container. Add your soil horizons in this order: rocks, gravel, sand, soil. As you add each layer, mark the top of it on the masking tape strip.

Push the potato masher into the soil, handle first, until it reaches the mark where the soil met the sand. Hold the container steady and try balancing a book on the masher.

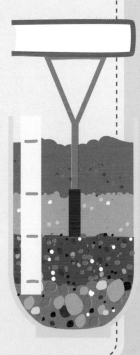

Make a note of what happens. Push the masher deeper into the soil. Can you balance a book now? Can you add more books? How far do you have to push the masher before it becomes stable?

Different Soil for Different Climates

Climate is the average weather in a place over a long time. A desert climate is dry, as it hardly ever rains there. When it rains, it is rainy for that day, but it is still a dry climate. Temperature and rainfall influence soil formation. They affect how fast rocks weather and dead organisms decompose. Soils develop faster in warm, moist climates, and slowest in cold or dry ones.

Savanna

Savannas are open grasslands with few trees. The soils are not very **fertile**. Organic matter supplies some nutrients at the soil's surface, but it decays very quickly in the high temperatures and the soil drains quickly.

Tundra

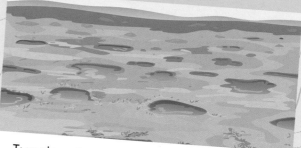

Tundra stays frozen for most of the year. There is little rain. The cold climate means the soil forms slowly, is shallow, and not very fertile. Plants only grow for a few weeks a year. Dead plants break down slowly, so soil contains a lot of undecomposed organic matter that forms a special kind of soil called peat. Peat helps our planet by storing carbon.

Rain forest

A rain forest is a tall, dense jungle with a lot of rainfall. Little light reaches the forest floor, so plants grow slowly. Rotting leaves and twigs, warm temperatures, and high rainfall help form a deep soil. Long tree roots also break up rock, which adds nutrients.

HANDS-ON

What Climate Are You?

Do some research. Can you find out what climate your region has? See if you can find out what plants grow best in your area. Look at local weather maps for information, and ask any gardener or farmer friends.

What Is Climate Change?

Climate change is a long term change in the general weather conditions, such as temperature and rainfall, experienced on Earth. Earth is experiencing climate change now. Ice is melting faster than usual, sea levels are rising, and flowers and plants are blooming at unusual times. Certain gases in our atmosphere trap heat and keep it from escaping. Known as the **greenhouse effect**, these gases warm Earth like a greenhouse keeps plants warm. Soil and plants help fight climate change. They capture the harmful gas, carbon dioxide, that causes the greenhouse effect.

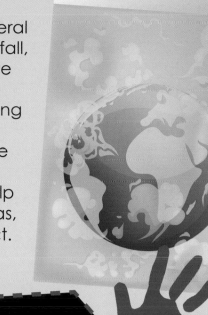

BE A SOIL GEOLOGIST
Create Different Forest Biomes

You Will Need:

adult help needed

- two plastic bottles
- some small rocks
- compost
- a measuring cup
- some water
- two large ziplock bags
- a marker
- a pencil
- notebook

The Geology:

Your "sunny" biome is like a **temperate** forest. Your "shady" biome is a rain forest. A temperate climate has mild temperatures. Most of Europe and North America are temperate.

How to Creat Your Climates:

Ask an adult to help cut two plastic bottles in half. Place an inch (2.5 cm) of rocks in each bottom half. Then add a 2-inch (5 cm) layer of compost. Poke three fingernail-deep holes in the compost in both bottles. Plant a seed in each hole and cover them with soil.

Water the soil until water starts to appear around the rocks. The soil should be just moist. Note how much water you needed. Place each bottle in a ziplock bag and seal them. With a marker, write "sunny" on one bag and "shady" on the other. Place the sunny bag on a sunny windowsill. Place the other bag in a very warm, shady place.

Record the day and time in a notebook. Observe the bags at the same time each day and make notes. Measure the seedlings as they grow. Which climate grows the best seedlings?

Sandy Soils

You can usually tell sandy soil by its pale color and dry feel. Sandy soils are light soils, as they don't have much heavy clay in them. They are quicker to warm up than clay soils. The large grains in sandy soil means water drains easily through the gaps. This means sandy soil dries out very quickly and nutrients get washed away. Because of this, many plants do not grow well in areas where soil is very sandy.

Mineral sand is made up of tiny grains of rock. Weathering breaks the rock into small pieces and **erosion** moves the grains along streams, rivers, and glaciers. Most sand is made from weathered quartz, found in granite. Quartz sand found in soil is rough and angular. Beach and desert sand transported long distances by water or wind will be rounder.

HANDS-ON

Examine Sandy Soil

Take a close look at some sandy soil using a magnifying glass or microscope. Can you see grains of sand in the soil? What color are they? Can you guess what type of rock the grains might have come from?

HANDS-ON Sandy Soil Test

An easy way to tell if your soil is sandy is to try this test. Take a handful of soil and wet it. It should be wet enough to start to stick together, but not stick to your hand. Now roll your soil sample into a small ball. Place the ball down on a flat surface. If the ball falls apart, you have very sandy soil!

BE A SOIL GEOLOGIST
Make Incredible Waterproof Sand!

You Will Need:

- shoe waterproofing spray or fabric protector
- a baking sheet
- aluminum foil
- sand
- a spoon
- a bowl of water

The Geology:

Scientists think waterproof sand could help grow crops in sandy soil. How? By keeping water from draining away. A layer of waterproof sand below the roots holds moisture where it is needed. Treated sand can also clean ocean oil spills! It soaks up floating oil and then sinks, making oil easier to remove.

How to Make It:

Cover your baking sheet with foil. Spread the sand in a thin layer over the foil. Go outside. Spray the sand with waterproofing spray, then wait around 15 minutes for the sand to dry. Stir it with a spoon, spread it out, and spray it again. Repeat this three to four times until your sand is coated on all sides. Test a sample by dropping a little water on it. If the water soaks into your sample, add more spray.

Slowly pour the sand into a bowl of water. Can you shape the sand into a sandcastle? Ordinary sand can't be molded into shapes underwater. Now scoop a handful of the molded sand out of the water. What happens?

Amazing Clay

Gardeners and farmers may not like clay soil. Why? Clay stays wet and cold in winter. It stays wet because the spaces between clay particles are tiny, so water can't easily pass through. Wet soil takes a long time to warm up. Once it has warmed, it dries and cracks in the hot weather. It may not be the best soil for growing things, but it does have many other uses.

Think About This...

Why would very wet soil be bad for growing plants?

Making Things from Clay

People have been building houses and making pottery using clay soil for thousands of years. Bricks can be made from clay that is shaped and dried in the sun. Tiles and pottery are made by shaping and then heating the clay in a really hot fire.

HANDS-ON Finding Clay in Soil

You will need:
- a shovel
- a ruler

Make sure you ask permission first before you start digging any holes!

Most soil contains some clay. Dig a hole around 8 inches (20 cm) deep. Roll a handful of the soil from the hole into a sausage shape. Can you form it into a ring? If you can, the soil contains clay.

Or, you could do a drainage test to measure how quickly water will soak through the soil. Dig a hole around 12 inches (30 cm) deep by 12 inches (30 cm) wide. You might want to dig a few holes to find the best clay-rich soil. Fill the holes with water. Measure the water level every hour. Loam soil drains at around 2 inches (5 cm) per hour. If it drains less than 1 inch (2.5 cm), it is probably clay soil.

BE A SOIL GEOLOGIST
Make Your Own Clay Pot from Soil

You Will Need:

- two buckets
- some clay-rich soil
- an outdoor space
- some string
- a large square of old cloth with a fine weave, such as an old cotton sheet

adult help needed

The Geology:

Clay is formed when molten rock under Earth's surface become solid rock, which then breaks down into a fine-grained soil. Usually the top layer of an area of clay is best for pottery. The bottom layers will have other rock in them, and will crumble.

How to Make Them:

Outside, fill a bucket one-third full of clay soil. Top up the bucket with water, until two-thirds full. Break up the soil with your hands and leave it to soak for an hour. Break up the soil again, and stir. Then let the soil settle for a few minutes. Any rocks and sand will separate from the clay and settle to the bottom.

Ask someone to help you hold a large cloth over the second bucket. If your cloth has a loose weave, fold it in half. Carefully pour the clay mixture into the cloth. When rocks or sand reach the edge of the bucket, stop pouring. Lift the corners of the cloth to form a bag . Tie it tightly with string. Hang the bag outside to drip for two days. If your clay is still wet, knead it into a ball and leave it in the sunshine. The clay can be stored in a bag.

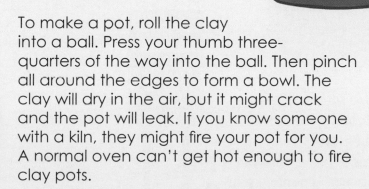

To make a pot, roll the clay into a ball. Press your thumb three-quarters of the way into the ball. Then pinch all around the edges to form a bowl. The clay will dry in the air, but it might crack and the pot will leak. If you know someone with a kiln, they might fire your pot for you. A normal oven can't get hot enough to fire clay pots.

Is Your Soil Acidic or Alkaline?

Whether your soil is acidic or alkaline can affect what can grow in it. We measure how acidic or alkaline things are using a scale known as the **pH scale**. On this 14-point scale, zero is very acidic, and 14 means very alkaline. Ideally, soil is close to the middle of the scale, just slightly acidic, at a pH of around 6.5.

NEUTRAL

ACIDIC   0 1 2 3 4 5 6 7 8 9 10 11 12 13 14   ALKALINE

Think About This... ?

Vinegar is an acid. Many cleaning products are alkalis. What common liquid do you think might be a **neutral** 7 on the pH scale, neither acid nor alkali?

What causes soil to be acidic or alkaline?

Rainfall is slightly acidic. It becomes even more acidic when certain gases are in our air. These gases can come from pollution, lightning, or volcanic eruptions. Plant roots, decaying plants, and fertilizer can make soil acidic, too. An area's local rock influences the soil's pH. Rock containing quartz, shale, and coal can produce acidic soil.

Soil in dry areas is often alkaline. Pollution, ash, fertilizers, and water softeners can all cause alkaline soil. Local chalk and limestone rock produce alkaline soil.

HANDS-ON Do a Soil pH Test

You will need:
- a soil pH meter
- pen and paper

pH

If you have a gardener friend or family member, they may have a soil pH meter. Follow the meter's instructions. They usually have probes that you push into the soil. Test different areas. Keep notes of your soil tests in a notebook.

If soil pH is less than 6.5, it is considered acidic. More than 7.3 is considered alkaline. In between is neutral soil.

BE A SOIL GEOLOGIST
What pH Soil Is Best for Growing?

You Will Need:

- pH testing strips
- three plastic cups
- three large, empty soda bottles
- a large bottle of distilled water
- lemon juice and baking soda
- a ruler
- some fast-sprouting seeds
- some soil

The Geology:

A soil's pH affects which nutrients can be taken up by plants. Some plants prefer a different pH than others, depending on what nutrients they need. Most plants like a value of around 6.5. Potatoes like a pH of about 5. Peanuts, parsley, and strawberries like a pH of about 5.5.

There are materials you can add to soil to change the pH. Sulfur lowers the pH and makes soil more acidic. Lime raises the pH and makes soil more alkaline.

How to Test It:

Rinse the soda bottles well. Fill each bottle three-quarters full with the distilled water.

Now you need to prepare your water bottles so each contains water with a different pH value. We will create water with pH values of 2, 7, and 9. Distilled water is already neutral and has a value of 7, so simply label one bottle "7". For your acidic water we want a value of pH 2. Add lemon juice to the water, a drop at a time. Test the water with a testing strip. Keep adding lemon juice until your strip matches the color by the 2 on the strip's color chart. Label the bottle "2".

For your alkaline water, pH 9, add tiny amounts of baking soda. Test the water as before, and label the bottle "9" when you get the desired color

Fill each drinking cup with soil and plant three seeds in each. Label each cup 2, 7, and 9. Lightly water each cup every day using the bottle with the same number. Keep the bottles and cups in the same conditions.

Observe and take notes. Measure the plants' growth and make a chart. Which plant grew the best?

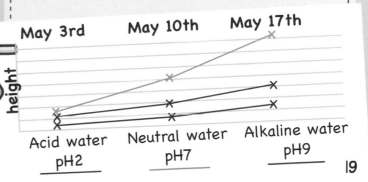

Can Soil Really Clean Water?

If you were asked to clean some murky water, you probably wouldn't think to use mud! But actually, soil is nature's water filter. When water passes through soil, the soil picks up impurities such as animal waste and chemicals.

Wetlands are amazing water filters. Wetland soil drains very slowly. The soil removes metals in water and traps **sediment** and **nitrogen**. Wetland plants act as living filters, trapping sediment and nutrients. In Florida, scientists have specially built a wetland to filter fertilizer from water heading toward the Everglades!

HANDS-ON Does Particle Size Matter?

You will need:
adult help needed

- scissors
- some water
- a glass
- some glitter
- 2 small plastic bottles
- gravel and topsoil
- aluminum foil
- rubber band
- paper towel

Never wash glitter down the drain. Throw glittery soil and gravel in the trash. Filter the glitter out of the water using paper towel.

Does the size of soil particles affect how well soil filters water? Try this simple experiment. Ask an adult to help you cut the top third from two plastic bottles. Take off the lid. Cover the bottle's opening with foil. Poke some small holes in the foil and secure it with a rubber band.

Fill one bottle's top with gravel, and the second with some soil. Rest the tops upside down on the bottle bottoms. Mix some glitter into a glass of water. Pour some water into both bottles. What do you think will happen? Which filter was fastest? Did you see glitter in the water from both bottles at the end of the experiment? Or just one? Or neither? What does that tell you?

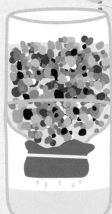

Think About This... ?

If the speed that water travels through soil affects how well the soil filters water, which soil type do you think would filter water the best?

silt

sand

clay

BE A SOIL GEOLOGIST
Build a Soil Water Treatment Plant

You Will Need:

adult help needed

- some muddy water
- a small plastic bottle
- 1 tablespoon alum
- some fine sand, coarse sand, and small pebbles, all rinsed clean
- a coffee filter
- a rubber band
- a large spoon

The Geology:

To treat our water, we used four processes:
- Stirring and pouring the water adds air and allows gases to escape.
- The alum sticks any solid particles together in clumps, which helps make the water clear.
- Gravity pulls particles to the bottom of the container.
- Filtering the water separates any last solid particles from the water.

Water treatment plants also use chemicals to remove bacteria and microorganisms. IMPORTANT – Our water is not safe to drink, as it did not undergo that final process.

How to Make It:

Ask an adult to cut the top third from a plastic bottle, or reuse a bottle from page 16. Stir the muddy water with a spoon until mixed thoroughly. Add a tablespoon of alum to the water. Slowly stir the water for five minutes, then leave it to settle for 20 minutes.

Secure a coffee filter to the bottle's opening using a rubber band. Put the bottle top upside down in the bottle's bottom. Now add filtration layers – first a layer of pebbles, then the coarse sand, and a layer of fine sand on top.

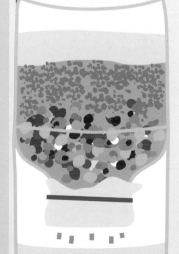

Now, pour some of the muddy water through the treatment plant. Once the water has filtered through, compare the remaining muddy water with the filtered water. Do they look and smell different?

BE A SOIL GEOLOGIST
Soil and Water Experiments

You Will Need:

- a sponge
- some water
- a large bowl
- a cup
- a pencil and paper

Soil acts much like a sponge. Try these experiments using a sponge and water and learn some amazing facts about absorbent soil.

Can Water in Soil Travel Upward?

Put around half an inch (1.2 cm) of water in a bowl. Put a dry sponge in the bowl. Only the bottom of the sponge should be in the water. Note down what happens. Has your sponge soaked up water to a level higher than the water level?

The Geology:

Why does water go up the sponge? Water molecules stick to the sponge, and stick to each other. As one water molecule travels up the tiny holes in the sponge, it draws the others with it. This is how plants pull water from the soil up their stems. The process is known as **capillary action**.

Does Wet Soil Still Contain Air?

See if you can saturate your sponge so there is no air left in the holes. With your sponge still in the bowl, pour water over it until it is completely full of water. Now squeeze your sponge under the water. Can you see air bubbles?

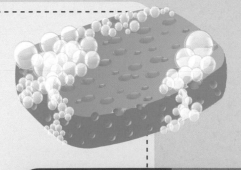

The Geology:

Soil is like a sponge. It has lots of tiny holes that can soak up water. Even soaked soil will still have a little air trapped in the tiny holes between particles.

Think About This... ?

Why is it good to have some air in the soil?

What Happens to Saturated Soil?

Squeeze a sponge and hold it over a bowl. Slowly pour water on the sponge until it is **saturated**. When the sponge can't hold any more, water will pour out of the bottom due to the force of gravity.

The Geology:

Like the sponge, when soil can't hold any more water, the water drains down toward the bedrock, taking any nutrients with it.

What Is Runoff?

Hold a sponge flat over a bowl. Slowly pour water onto it. The water will soak into the top and gravity will pull the water downward. Now hold the sponge at an angle over the bowl. Pour water quickly onto the sponge. The water will flow across the surface and not soak in. This is known as runoff.

The Geology:

If water falls onto the soil quite slowly, the water will soak in. As the soil gets wetter, the large pores are not able to hold the water, so water moves down through the soil. When water is quickly added to the soil, such as by heavy rain, water flows across the surface of the soil.

What Is a Water Table?

Place a saturated sponge in an empty bowl. Pour a cup of water over it and leave it for an hour to settle. The level of water in your bowl now is like the soil's water table. It is the level below which the soil is completely saturated.

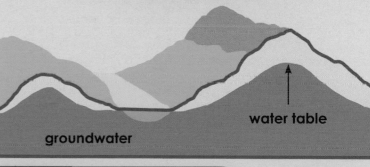

water table

groundwater

When all possible water has drained from soil by gravity, the soil is said to be at **field capacity**. Clay holds the most water at field capacity, and sand holds the least.

The Geology:

Water tables rise and fall depending on how much rain or sunshine an area has. Water below the water table is called groundwater. People often drill down to find and use groundwater.

23

What Lives in the Soil?

Under our feet, the soil is home to all kinds of creatures, from microscopic microbes to large burrowing animals. Some animals live underground for protection. Others depend on the soil for their food.

Plant roots and fungi grow in soil. One huge fungus in Oregon has tendrils that spread 2.4 miles (3.8 km) underground!

Beetles, spiders, ants, millipedes – hundreds of creepy-crawlies live underground. They improve the soil by creating air holes and shredding organic material.

Moles, rabbits, and some other mammals make burrows in the soil. Moles find their food underground. They eat earthworms. Other mammals, such as rabbits, eat plants, but use the soil as a safe place to hide.

There are over 7,000 species of earthworms. One type of Australian earthworm grows to 3.3 feet (1 m) long! Earthworms are great gardeners. They help break up soil and move water around.

Some things living in soil are so tiny you can only see them through a microscope. These creatures are called microbes. There are more microbes in a handful of soil than there are people living on Earth!

HANDS-ON Do A Creepy-Crawly Count

You will need:

- an area you can dig
- a shovel
- two buckets
- a garden sieve or mesh
- a notebook and pencil

Ask permission to dig a small hole outside. Put the fresh soil in a bucket. Place a garden sieve or mesh over a second bucket. Pour the soil onto the sieve, a little at a time. Most of the soil should fall through, and any worms, beetles, and other living things will stay on top of the mesh. Make a note of the numbers and different species you find. Then carefully put them back where you found them.

BE A SOIL GEOLOGIST
How Do Worms Help Our Soil?

You Will Need:

- some different-colored soils
- a very large see-through tub or bottle with lid
- some earthworms
- some dead leaves
- water
- a notebook and pencil

adult help needed

IMPORTANT - Do not use peat or pure sand in this experiment, as they might harm your earthworms.

How to Make Your Wormery:

Ask an adult to help you poke some holes around the top of your container. Add your soil, one color at a time, taking care not to mix the layers. If the soil is dry, add a little water. The soil should be moist but not soaking wet. Place a layer of dead leaves at the surface.

Place the earthworms on the leaves and put on the lid. Leave the container in a cool spot. Record what happens to the soil layers each day for a month. Write notes, make drawings, or take photographs. At the end of your experiment, put the earthworms back where you found them.

The Geology:

The earthworms will usually pull the dead leaves down into the soil. They will also mix the layers of soil as they move from one layer to another.

Good Microbes and Bad Microbes

Living things are made up of tiny parts called cells. We have millions of cells, but some microbes are so tiny they are made of only a single cell! You can only see microbes when they group together. Green, slimy algae on soil is made up of thousands of microbes.

Some microbes are good for the soil and plants, and some microbes cause harm.

Microbes break down organic matter, rocks, and minerals, releasing nutrients into the soil. They help turn nitrogen in the atmosphere into nutrients too.

Microbes create little tunnels in the soil. The holes create space for air and water.

Microbes can carry diseases that make plants, people, and animals ill.

Think About This... ?

Some bacteria create the gas **oxygen**. Why would that help people and animals?

Some microbes release antibiotics that help protect the roots of plants from disease.

HANDS-ON Prove Your Soil Has Microbes!

You will need:

- a cotton sock
- a nylon or polyester sock
- a shovel
- a stick

Microbes help decompose things in soil. They can even eat through cotton! Fill a cotton sock and a nylon sock with soil and bury them around 6 inches (15.2 cm) below the surface. Mark the spot with a stick. Leave them for around 8 weeks. What has happened to the cotton sock when you dig it up? If it is full of holes, you have microbes in your soil. Microbes cannot break down the plastics in nylon and polyester.

Soil and the Carbon Cycle

Soil, especially peat and wetland soil, helps take carbon from our atmosphere. Carbon dioxide gas (CO_2) is one of the gases that create the harmful greenhouse effect. Humans and animals breathe out carbon dioxide. Plants take carbon dioxide out of the atmosphere. After a plant or animal dies, it releases carbon into the air, soil, and water. Microbes in soil feed on the dead plant or animal, creating carbon dioxide. Carbon dioxide gas goes back up into the atmosphere. Any remaining carbon is stored in the soil.

BE A SOIL GEOLOGIST
Watch Microbes at Work

You Will Need:

- some soil
- limewater (from a drugstore)
- eye protection
- jar with a lid
- small container
- a pencil and notebook

adult help needed

The Geology:

The limewater will turn chalky when carbon dioxide gas mixes with it. If your limewater has turned a milky white, then your soil must contain carbon dioxide-producing microbes!

How to Do the Experiment:

Ask an adult to help you with this experiment. IMPORTANT - Limewater can damage your eyes and skin, so wear eye protection and gloves.

Half fill the jar with garden soil. Put on the gloves and eye protection. Pour a little limewater into the small container. Place the uncovered container on the layer of soil in the jar. Put the lid on the jar. Make a note of what the limewater looked like.

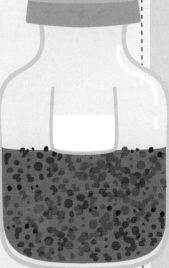

Every day, examine the limewater. Has its appearance changed? Make a note of what the limewater looks like. After three days you should notice it change, if your soil has enough microbes.

27

Why Soil Wears Away

Soil erosion is the gradual destruction and removal of soil in a particular area by rivers, the sea, overfarming, or the weather. When the soil erodes, land becomes bare and nothing will grow.

Flat land

Soil forms as quickly as it is lost, protected from erosion by trees and plants. The roots hold the soil together belowground. Aboveground, leaves act as a windbreak and protect against heavy rain. Trees and plants are often cleared for farming. Plowing or allowing too many animals to graze can cause land to become bare. Once the land is bare, the wind can blow the soil away.

Slopes

On flat land or gentle slopes, soil is usually formed as quickly as it erodes. That is not the case on sloping land. Soil will wash away much more quickly on hillsides. The soil ends up in rivers and is washed out to sea. Plowing the soil on slopes can cause the earth to become bare, because each time the soil is lifted it moves a little way down the slope.

Think About This... ?

Why do your think farmers in ancient Peru created these terraced areas in the mountains?

28

HANDS-ON How Does Water Erode Soil?

You will need:

- a few books
- a baking sheet
- some dry sand
- a large bowl
- some water
- a teaspoon

Place one edge of the baking sheet over the edge of the bowl and the other edge propped up on some books to form a slope. Place a mound of sand in the middle of the sheet. Slowly drip some water onto the mound. Does any sand wash down the hillside? What happens if you pour the water onto the sand? Try the same experiment with wet sand. Does it erode faster or slower?

BE A SOIL GEOLOGIST
How Does Wind Erode Soil?

You Will Need:

adult help needed

- an outside area
- a hair dryer
- eye protection
- a protractor
- some dry sand
- a baking sheet
- a cardboard box
* a notepad and pencil
- some water and some gravel

How to Make a Wind Tunnel:

Put on your eye protection. Go outside. Place a pile of dry sand on the baking sheet, then place it in the opening of the cardboard box. The box will catch any flying sand. Hold the hair dryer at an angle of around 45 degrees around 4 inches (10 cm) from the sand. You can check the angle using a protractor. Turn the hair dryer on low for 30 seconds. Record what happens. If nothing happens, turn the dryer up to medium or high.

How can you slow erosion? Rebuild your sand mound. Add things you think may help slow the process. Make notes about what worked and what didn't.

The Geology:

Sand grains are easily eroded by wind. To slow down erosion, add some water or small stones.

Glossary

acid   a compound that usually dissolves in water, has a sour taste, and turns litmus paper red.

alkali   a salt or mixture of salts easily dissolved in water and present in some soils of very dry regions.

atmosphere   the whole volume of air surrounding Earth.

auger   a tool made like a screw used for boring holes or moving loose material.

biome   a region with a certain climate and certain types of living things.

capillary action   the ability of a liquid to flow in narrow spaces without the assistance of, or even against, external forces like gravity.

carbon   a nonmetallic element found more or less pure in nature.

carbon dioxide   a heavy, colorless gas, formed especially by the burning and breaking down of organic substances, that is absorbed from the air by plants.

chemicals   substances such as elements or compounds obtained from a chemical process or used to get a chemical result.

climate   the average weather conditions of a particular place or region over a period of many years.

crust   the outer part of Earth.

decomposing   breaking down through biological activity (for example, by bacteria) into simpler chemical substances.

erosion   the process of wearing away by the action of water, wind, or glacial ice.

fertile   producing vegetation or crops plentifully.

field capacity   the amount of soil moisture or water content held in soil after excess water has drained away.

limestone   a rock formed from animal remains (as shells or coral) that consists mainly of calcium carbonate.

microbes   organisms such as bacteria of microscopic or less-than-microscopic size.

minerals   solid chemical compounds that occur naturally in the form of crystals.

neutral   neither acid nor alkaline.

nitrogen   a colorless, tasteless, odorless element that occurs as a gas. It makes up 78 percent of Earth's atmosphere and forms a part of all living tissues.

nutrients   substances that provide nourishment essential for the maintenance of life and for growth.

olivine   a usually greenish mineral that is a silicate of magnesium and iron.

organic matter   plant and animal matter at various stages of decomposition, and cells and tissues of soil microbes.

organisms   living things that have organs which have separate functions but are dependent on each other.

oxygen   a colorless, tasteless, odorless gas that forms about 21 percent of Earth's atmosphere, and is necessary for life.

particles   one of the very small parts of matter.

pH scale   a scale used to specify the acidity or alkalinity of a solution.

saturated   unable to absorb or dissolve any more of a substance.

sediment   material such as stones and sand deposited by water, wind, or glaciers.

silt   a soil made from very small particles of sediment from water.

weathering   the action of the forces of nature that changes exposed rocks, minerals, and soil.

wetlands   land or areas (as marshes or swamps) that are flooded either permanently or seasonally.

Further Information

Museums and Places to Visit

Visitors' centers. Your area may have wetlands, peat bogs, clay deposits, or desert visitor centers where you can find out about local soil types.

Visit local farms. Farmers are very knowledgeable about the soil. There may be farmers in your area that would help you learn all about soil.

Contact garden centers, gardening clubs, or community gardens. You might be able to find out what people grow in your area, and find useful equipment such as pH tester kits.

Useful Websites

This Soil Science Society of America website is packed with information, including information about each state's soil profile.
https://www.soils4kids.org/about

This Learning Junction animated video teaches about soil layers.
https://www.youtube.com/watch?v=og9A_Apr534

The Audobon Society has a list of interesting facts about dirt.
https://www.audubon.org/news/10-incredible-facts-about-dirt

Books to Read

Graham, Ian. *You Wouldn't Want to Live Without Dirt!* London, UK: Franklin Watts, 2016.

Stroud, Jackie, Dr. *Under Your Feet. Soil, Sand, and Everything Underground.* London, UK: DK Children, 2020.

Publisher's note to parents and teachers: Our editors have reviewed the websites listed here to make sure they're suitable for students. However, websites may change frequently. Please note that students should always be supervised when they access the internet.

Index